The Technique of the

By RAYMUND ANDREA, K.R.

Grand Master, AMORC, Great

▽ ▽ ▽ ▽ ▽

*The Mystic Triangle
November 1927*

I NEITHER propose to ask permission of, nor to render any apology to, our friends the Theosophists for writing intimately in our Rosicrucian magazine of the Master Kut-Hu-Mi. The publication in our magazine a few months ago of the Master's photograph, with a list declaring his very prominent position in the hierarchy of the Masters and the extent of his great authority in world activities, no doubt came as a considerable surprise to a large number of our friends, who had hitherto regarded the Master as exclusively concerned in the affairs of their Society and themselves as the main objective of his personal interest. I write in all seriousness, for there have existed the strongest reasons for the creation of this impression. However, the illusion on this head has passed, and it is now practically demonstrated that the Master is far too universal a character, and too versatile in activity, to confine his unique influence to any group of aspirants of a single name. Indeed, it is surprising how such an idea of limitation and exclusive interest should ever have been entertained by any well-informed occult student. The most simple application of the law of analogy should dissipate this error. The objective of the aspirant in his studies is to transcend the personal attitude, to observe his and his fellowmen from a Cosmic standpoint, to offer his hand in help wherever the cry of man reaches his ear; what then would he expect to be the invariable attitude of the Master whom he aspires to meet and be assisted by on the path to liberation? Is not the Master the Compassionate One who has given all for the world, and can perfect compassion exclude, or be bound by a name? Does not the scripture say: "When the pupil is ready the Master appears?" I am firmly of the opinion that when we become fully initiated into the superphysical and enter, in full consciousness, into the secret assemblies and councils of the Masters, we shall be not a little surprised at the diverse nationalities and the manifold types and the independent status of the pupils there contacted and engaged unitedly in world service under that august supervision. Perhaps no other experience will so quickly and effectually divest us of this mean bondage to locality and name, nor so readily enable us to attain that comprehensive and catholic view which is the note of the truly occult mind.

In the light of the increasing information vouchsafed us in our day of the Masters and their work, we may take a bold and decisive step toward an entirely fresh adjustment of outlook regarding their personality and procedure. The old—yes, ridiculous and conceited—idea of a great world worker, such as a Master of Occultism, devoting his transcendent powers and wisdom to fostering exclusively the dreams of a small group of aspirants gathered around the one or two accredited pupils to whom, at that time, he embraced an opportunity, under the law of Karma, of making known his activities to the Western world, must go. It no doubt served a good purpose, inasmuch as it gave a considerable importance to those who entertained the new knowledge, imparted a consciousness of exclusive adoption and of individual worth, and urged them to unusual activity in disseminating it. We today recognize the importance of our mission, we need the consciousness of individual worth and the incentive to unusual activity, but we know nothing of exclusive adoption. The voice of the Masters is an impersonal one: that is the cardinal fact for us; and he who can respond to that voice is known and accepted, whoever and wherever he may be. The swift movement of events during recent years, the increasing complexity of human life and relationships, the resolute pioneer work in the realms of mind, the amazing progress in the great fields of scientific discovery, and the emergence of the psychic on every hand, are all strong indications, for those who have the eyes to see, of hierarchical response to the demands of the growing soul. The old dividing lines have vanished. The cry is: Onward in the name of the soul! The man with that irrepressible passion deep in the heart is *known*, whether he hide himself in the solitudes or among men; he is known to the Master who is a world focus of the same constraining passion. The two are one under the occult law—the law which is perfected in the technique of the Master.

Few subjects are so profound and fascinating as that of the technique of the Master. It is with certain phases of the technique of the Master Kut-Hu-Mi that I propose to deal. He has been well named "the Illustrious." He is presented to us as of singular and majestic mien, with a lustre and dignity of personality edifying to behold. In the clear and tranquil light of the mesmeric eyes we discern the concentration and completion of human experience. It is a blessed thought that the Higher Powers have given such men to humanity, comparatively unknown but ever watchful, to guide and inspire it, through the agency of their disciples, along the difficult path of evolution. With all its trials and sufferings, life affords no greater privilege to man than to be consciously active in some aspect of this endeavour. But the technique of the Master is not easy to understand or to translate into life. He knows too well the extreme rigor of his laws to demand from any soul what it has not yet found the power and insight to give. For the first step is an entirely spontaneous one and the offspring of a high order of vibration which is the culmination of a mature experience in the knowledge of the planes. This experience is often not an acquirement of the present incarnation, but exists as subjective memory. The history of its direct attainment is hidden in the past and is now chiefly shown in swift and versatile response to occult truth in any form, accompanied with exceptional ability of some nature for the expression of that truth. Wherever this response exists, and is of a pure and powerful character, there we may discern the silent influence of the Master's realm upon an awakening soul in the far time. He is now ready for the technique of the Master. There will be for him, in the scripture of wisdom, a geometry of the Spirit which he will delight to ponder and apply to the infinite intricacies of life and character. Humanity, passing and repassing between the two eternities, will no longer appear to him as an uninteresting pageant and unrelated to himself: the power and passion of its living blood will create a mighty music in his soul, often very hard to be borne. Vibrant harmonies will arise within and sweep to celestial heights; strange chords of sombre pitch will mingle with his song of life; and the keen breath of a superhuman strength must have touched both heart and brain to enable him to stand before the knowledge that this symphony of a thousand voices of joy and sorrow is indeed his own collective Karma, in martial array, opening the gates of self-cognition. It is the Master's response to the soul's endeavour; it is the Master's technique demonstrating within him, whose inexorable law is: That every latent germ of good and bad in his temperament shall be awakened and declare itself.

Many are the misgivings of an aspirant when that law begins to operate in his personal sphere. Well may he think that far from making the smooth progress expected, he is on the path of retrogression. "It is not enough," says the Master, "to know thoroughly what the chela is capable of doing or not doing at the time and under the circumstance during probation. We have to know of what he may be capable under different and every kind of opportunities." A stern and exacting law of which the world knows nothing! Therefore the aspirant must be perfectly ready and willing to withstand its criticism. There is nothing intentionally mystifying in the procedure; it is simply a procedure which runs counter to all other procedures he is conversant with and for which he has to develop a rare discrimination. It cannot reasonably be expected that he will be intrusted with new and altogether higher responsibilities in a totally different realm of mentation and action, unless he has been drastically probed and tested by the searching influences proceeding from that superior realm. New faculties emerge under stress; not in the unexercised nature of him who fears the consequences of self-discovery. There is no smooth and easy path of ascent here; and with that assurance the aspirant must be prepared to find the confidence which the Master will certainly demand in him for the initial trials.

A member recently wrote me in these words: "Sometimes I feel further than ever from this attunement. I wonder why it is. I have an idea, probably gathered from my reading, that while one does not make any effort in this direction consciously there are influences at work which keep things balanced for you. You have your ups and downs. But once you begin making conscious effort these forces are upset and you may have all ups, or you may have all downs. You might easily make a great mess of the whole affair. I know at the moment my mind feels just in that state with regard to everything." How exactly, though quite unconsciously, does this member shadow forth the fact of the initial experience referred to! In her case it has not been delayed; her work in the occult field has been of short duration, and in the work of our Order she has only advanced to the third National grade. But there is no *time* in this realm. We are dealing with the intangible self, pregnant with undelivered Karma, and the word of knowledge of the right vibrational value may be all-sufficient to precipitate a phase of circumstance, perplexing and painful, but written largely in Nature's great law, and which must be met and understood. It is the *conscious effort* made to progress on the path which is the determining factor. Until that moment life moves slowly onward at its accustomed pace; there is an established rhythm in the vehicles which imparts a relative sense of ease and adjustment in the various contacts of life; the furniture of the mind is well-known and thoroughly catalogued, the selection considered excellent and becoming, nothing eccentric, nothing revolutionary, nothing at variance with the preconceived scheme, nothing to disturb the aesthetic taste of its possessor. But alas! the counterfeit peace of stagnation and conformity is not for the pioneer; the tidal wave of evolution will surely agitate the still waters in good time and compel advancement. And if, through fervent aspiration to the divine, the aspirant deliberately seeks the feet of the Master, sooner or later the trial comes to the soul, and well for him who, even through disappointment and tears, recognizes the guiding hand and clasps it in perfect faith. For the Master has said: "The mass of human sin and frailty is distributed throughout the life of man who is content to remain an average mortal. It is gathered in and concentrated, so to say, within one period of the life of a chela—the period of probation."

A large percentage of our members are wrestling with the difficulties incident to the period of probation. It is the period paramount, wherein the technique of the Master is so unexpected and penetrating that the aspirant's intention must be at once steadfast, pure and spiritual, to intuitionally grasp and personalize it. One has constantly to confront the lamentations of aspirants who do not appear to realize that occult progress must be slow, and that trials met and overcome are of the very essence of advancement. "The iron rule is," says the Master, "that what powers one gets he must himself acquire."—"He must not even desire too earnestly or too passionately the object he would reach; else the very wish will prevent the possibility of its fulfilment." The aspirant is working *upon himself,* upon the texture of his vehicles of expression, not upon external matter, as an artist fashioning material after his own conception. He has been so accustomed, in the physical world, to impose his will objectively upon men and things and receive an immediate response, that it is long before he comprehends that the deeper laws of the psychic and spiritual are alien to this. *There is no time in occultism.* The liquidation of Karma transpires in accordance with an inner law which is not in our will to hasten or delay. That is why the voice of the Masters, though often foreboding and tinged with warning, is ever a voice of encouragement; he knows that the persistent and courageous spirit will ultimately triumph over all. Has he not, as mortal man, himself triumphed? In every aspirant there is that which is akin to the Master's own immortal nature; the vital, dominant, irresistible seed of immortality which is destined to blossom into adeptship. But adeptship is a starry altitude supremely difficult of attainment. At every step of the way the Master has progressed scientifically and spiritually under the stern imposition of iron rule; obviously, then, no one better equipped than he to involve and guide the aspirant through the manifold intricacies of that rule, imperative for his complete knowledge and mastery of personal forces. Only through ceaseless application and after-pains incredible do the masters of the arts and sciences attain their superb insight and mastery, and inspire and redeem humanity from the commonplace and trivial, and entrance the dreaming idealist into ecstatic yearning for the Infinite. Only through steadfast service and never-failing aspiration, through love and compassion and sacrifice, through success and failure, through lonely vigil and impassioned admonition, through all the heights and depths of thought and emotion of which the eager heart and the awakened mind are capable, shall we gain a true perspective of the sure and perfect action, and become worthy exponents of the Master's technique.

We may expect a very marked characteristic in the aspirant as the result of consciously passing through such an eventful inner discipline: he will be spiritually positive. A passive character can never hope to handle the work of the Master. It is not in the nature of things. The master of art uses his vehicle or material of expression with power. He will undoubtedly be receptive to superior influences and often appear to be a tool in the hands of the genius of his art: but there is a world of difference between a highly cultured receptivity and a passivity without strength and poise. The Master is very direct on this matter: "It is not enough that you should set the example of a pure, virtuous life and a tolerant spirit; this is but negative goodness —and for chelaship will never do. You should —even as a simple member—learn that you may teach, acquire spiritual knowledge and strength that the weak may lean upon you, and the sorrowing victims of ignorance learn from you the cause and remedy of their pain." That is one of the hard sayings of occultism, but it must stand. Conventional goodness, and all the qualities which constitute a well-tempered character, are to be prized; but the aspirant who intends to take the stages of the occult path must possess, or must resolutely cultivate, a certain aggressiveness of spirit which compels every difficulty to yield its secret and grows stronger for the struggle. I speak to the aspirant who aspires to be a light and guide to others, who feels this deep call in his nature, who can take defeat in the arena of life and yet pass on, that thereby the qualifications for higher service may be born and raised to power within him. And one of the reasons for this insistance upon interior assertiveness is that we have to deal subjectively with powers and influences on other planes than the visible, which work actively into the personal life. "The aspirant is now assailed entirely upon the psychological side of his nature."--"The direct hostility of the Brothers of the Shadow always on the watch to perplex and haze the neophyte's brain" is not an imaginary menace. It is a Karmic heritage ranged along the path for opportune attack, before which the strong survive and the weak fall back. However keenly the sensitive nature may suffer and recoil before the inimical and unsuspected vibrations which impinge upon it, the inner self must have reached that measure of strength which can do and dare and be silent.

Through conscientious study of himself in the light of such reflections as these the aspirant comes to realize the full significance of the outworking of Karma in his life. On this matter he cannot be too rightly introspective and discriminative. The Master's comment is: "To unlock the gates of the mystery you must not only lead a life of the strictest probity, but learn to discriminate truth from falsehood. You have talked a great deal about Karma but have hardly realized the true significance of that doctrine. The time has come when you must lay the foundation of that strict conduct —in the individual as well as in the collective body—which, ever wakeful, guards against conscious as well as unconscious deception." His endeavour on the path will develop this discrimination and so clarify his vision that the truth of things will respond to his right-mindedness. For the Master *is* truth; he has no pleasure in the error of the aspirant: nor will he be subject to error if he persistently tries to identify his thinking with the thought of the Master. There is a pregnant admonition of the Master which he will profitably ponder: "My chelas must never doubt, nor suspect, nor injure our agents by foul thoughts. Our modes of action are strange and unusual, and but too often liable to create suspicion. The latter is a snare and a temptation. Happy is he whose spiritual perceptions ever whisper truth to him! Judge those directly concerned with us by that perception, not according to your worldly notions of things." That spiritual perception is the basis of everything. It will contradict much that the aspirant has always believed to be true, and he will experience pain in renouncing that which is so firmly woven into his world of facts. But his greatest help will be dogmatic faith, although his world crumble around him. There will be many a secret struggle, but the right aspirant scarcely troubles to count the cost.

And from this new strength indifference to opinion will arise. The aspirant must let appearances go. What his inmost heart dictates is the law, not the urgent voices of external authorities. The Master's word is: "He who damns himself in his own estimation and agreeably to the recognized and current code of honour to save a worthy cause may some day find out that he has reached thereby his loftiest aspirations. Selfishness and the want of self-sacrifice are the greatest impediments on the path of adeptship." Cannot we rest our cause implicitly on adept assurance? There can be no half measures in occultism. We either want the Master life or we do not: if

we do, there is but one law of conformity for us, and the technique of that law embraces every circumstance of life. It does not complicate, it simplifies life — if the necessary preparation has been taken. "What better cause for reward, what better discipline, than the daily and hourly performance of duty?"

The technique of the Master ramifies every phase of experience past and to come. It touches the inmost secret of his own supreme altitude and passes back to the common task of the present hour. Nothing is veiled to the eye of occult omniscience: no circumstance that cannot be divinely adjusted in the evolutionary scheme. We have to make the adjustment, whether in sorrow or in joy, and emerge more purified from the fire. "It is with armed hand, and ready to either conquer or perish, that the modern mystic can hope to achieve his object."
RAYMUND ANDREA.

Our Radio Work

▽ ▽ ▽ ▽ ▽

Since the last issue of the Triangle was sent forward we have installed the newer features of our radio equipment as announced in that issue. We are all prepared now to carry on international communications with our branches in any civilized land. The beautiful, highly efficient short-wave transmitter is a companion panel to the big panels of the broadcast equipment. This new section is so built and designed that it can be used for the transmission of code signals (dots and dashes) or phone (voice) on short waves. The great power used in this outfit makes possible daylight as well as night-time communication to almost every part of the civilized world, for we are using from five to ten times the power on this set that is used by those who communicate nightly with Europe.

On the evening of the first test, the practical value of it was demonstrated. The Imperator had just returned to Tampa from his trip to New York and Washington, and he had left Brother Kimmel in New York to attend to some official matters. He asked the operator of our long distance set to get in touch with Washington—not as a test of distance—but to make practical use of the outfit. A message was sent to Brother Kimmel, who had returned to his home in Washington, and in just seven minutes we had Brother Kimmel's reply. It took but three minutes to get the message into Brother Kimmel's sanctum at his home, and, with a lapse of one minute to prepare his answer, it took but three minutes to have the answer. Brother Kimmel has no short wave equipment in his home. How was it done? By sending our radio message to the radio representative in Washington, who immediately telephoned the message to Brother

Kimmel's home, waited for the answer and then put it on the air while we listened to each word as it was put on his antenna. Such service is quicker than by Western Union or Postal Telegraph. Our telegraph bills are a large item each month, and while our new radio equipment will not eliminate all of that —or even tend to lessen the expense of telegraphing—it will give us quicker and more private service. There is not a fair sized city or town in the United States or Canada, or a large city in any part of the world, that does not have a radio representative who can be reached by us and who will pass on to the right party by telephone or personal delivery a message which we may wish to send. Later we sent actual messages to members in New Zealand, Canada, Germany and France without any difficulty.

Since that first test was made we had a long talk over the air with the radio station at the Edgewater Hotel in Chicago and he reported that our tone and power were perfect and it was so easy to hear us and reach us that he would like to keep in touch with us nightly. Others in California and Canada and many States of the country answered our general "CQ" on the first test night and we were delighted.

The Government has granted to us a license, through the Federal Radio Commission, for this new section to our work, and our call letters for the present are 4ACY. These will be changed, as will our broadcast call letters, after we are located in California again.

Further plans about getting in radio communication with our branches several nights each week will be announced in a future issue.

▽ ▽ ▽ ▽ ▽
▽

The Technique of the Master

By Raymund Andrea

GRAND MASTER, AMORC, GREAT BRITAIN

▽ ▽ ▽ ▽ ▽

MEMBERS of our Order who are acquainted with the Theosophical text books will not be unaware that the founders of the Theosophical movement were considerably indebted to a Rosicrucian Brother of the Eastern Brotherhood, for instruction and personal guidance in connection with the problems associated with the carrying out of their mission. I refer to the Brother Serapis; and I have felt prompted to base the matter of this article on a quotation from one of his letters. It leads us to the heart of the subject of the Master's technique, a subject of unfailing interest and value to all of us, and one, moreover, upon which some members have asked me to write further because so many of the deepest problems contingent upon their progress along the path are bound up with it. Inevitably so, for the word of the Master is truth, and as we strenuously qualify through self understanding to work skillfully upon and with the souls of our fellow men, we become more and more possessed with the desire to see as he sees, speak as he speaks, do as he does, that our influence may become at last a living light to kindle the ready soul to self-recognition and larger purpose.

There is one important and palpable fact about the personal communications of the Masters, and that is, their complete and unassailable expression of the phase of truth under consideration. This may appear a truism, yet it is one for reflection. For instance, if we take the majority of text books on occultism we find that the exposition is fragmentary, subsequent text books along the same lines, at a later date, even from the pen of the same writer will—I do not say, annul the former ones—but necessitate considerable mental readjustments on the part of read-

ers. I need not specify cases, but any student of Theosophy can verify this statement. Further, such text books dealing with the same subject matter but from the hands of different writers are often very contradictory, and these divergencies in the exposition of occult truth are anything but satisfactory or helpful to the student. The positive assertions of these expositions, each so dogmatic and convincing in its way, appear equally to demand complete acceptance. If these different presentations were harmonious fragments, if they dovetailed into and corroborated each other, and formed one composite body of Cosmic truth, a very disturbing factor would be eliminated. Upon that one basis of sound and tested doctrine, the offspring of many advanced investigators in direct contact with one unimpeachable source of illumination, the student might well feel that he could ground his soul life with a deep sense of inner security. However the case is otherwise.

But when the Master speaks for the guidance of the soul we feel and know at once, and for all time, the indubitable certainty of his word. There is no need to compare it with any other utterances; no textbook is required to corroborate it. It is a phrase from Cosmic experience, and true to the experience of the evolving soul. We may not be ready to accept it now, but the time will come when we must accept it if we wish to advance. This indubitableness of the Master's word in its immediate or remote relationship to our human experience is a fact which always appeals to me as unique in literature. It is not difficult to see why it is never open to question or subject to qualification. There is no hidden depth of the soul which the Master has not sounded; no problem which he cannot instantly detach from every hampering consideration and observe it in the

clear, cool light of illuminated intellect. I use the term intellect intentionally, I see no reason for assuming, as many seem to assume, that the Master, because of his lofty spirituality, condescends not to use so poor a tool as intellect. Observe the vexations and perplexities that hedge round our problems because of the ever fluctuating and darkening shadows of the emotional and mental life, obstructing the clear light of the thinking principle, and raising a host of discordant vibrations which involve us in sore distress. The Master is entirely free from that. When he surveys the problem of the soul he stands above, not within it; it is reflected comprehensively and alone upon the clear and illuminated mirror of the intellect. He knows just what it means to us; he sees the defect of knowledge or foresight which gives it birth, the keen struggle of the soul to find a solution, or the resultant reactions upon our future growth. How often an aspirant questions the wisdom, justice, and compassion of the Master because the particular burden of life is not at once removed for the asking! But if the Master is a living example of adjusted Karmic forces every conceivable soul problem must be known to him, and he also knows the beneficient reactions of every Karmic problem which besets us. Why, we cannot behold the Master's countenance, or those of any of his high initiates, without discerning deeply charactered there the blessed memorials of manhood perfected through ancient suffering. It is this immense world experience, this agedness of the soul in the Master which vibrates in his word of guidance with such sombre emphasis, and holds us true to him even in the darkest hour. I have known a trembling soul to hang upon the Master's word when nothing in life or circumstance seemed to justify it; but the soul knew even though it could not understand, and that link of imperishable force and sympathy was all sufficient.

The necessity for specialized culture of the will in occult work is a matter upon which all of us are in full agreement. In all world progress it is the great driving force; but the will to tread the path is of a higher nature. It is in reality the inner spiritual self acting steadily and unceasingly through the personality. And when, through study and meditation, and one pointed determination to achieve masterhood, this inner self or spiritual will is gradually released and begins to act powerfully in the vehicles of the student, only then do the real problems of the path emerge and call for the greatest strength to deal with them. Then it is that many grow profoundly doubtful of their progress, and are ready to turn to the former relative security which was theirs. So long as we do not think too deeply or demand too much, the normal rhythm of life remains undisturbed; but to have thoroughly visualized the higher possibilities and sent forth a petition into the Master's realm to share in the responsibilities and blessings of a larger service, is a direct request of the soul to be subjected to that keener discipline which alone will make the greater service possible. And the student who is not yet sure of himself, who has not realized fully the depth and reality of his pledge of allegiance to the Higher Powers, is often greatly perplexed at the definite changes occurring in his mental life, and the altered aspect of circumstances. Yet this is but one of the tests which sooner or later confronts every student, and if the general trend of his life has not evolved a measure of strength and ripeness in his faculties he will be compelled to actively school himself in further world experience in order to successfully meet the test.

That life itself is the great initiator is a profound occult truth. It can be observed in the world of men every day. There are individuals around us who have no leaning toward the occult, yet so intense and varied are their labors, so strenuous and devoted are they in manifold works of ideal service for the race, that they have all the mental and inner equipment for rapidly passing the tests of the occult path. We have known many remarkable examples of this in the case of such individuals contacting the Order; and it brings to mind a statement in

The
Mystic
Triangle
February
1929

one of the early issues of our magazine: that the potentialities of a new member cannot be fully foreseen, and every care should be taken and encouragement given him in the early stages of the work in view of his possible great value and influence in the Order. In these men the will has reached its strength through long and versatile response in world experience; they stand at the point of mature mentality where they can receive the deeper knowledge of the soul; the sharp contacts and pain of life have rounded off a whole cycle of minor attachments and given them clear judgment, and a high degree of detachment from purely personal issues whereby they are able to bear the accelerated vibration which will eventuate when they take up the discipline of the path.

This is a factor for reflection. If the common experience of life has not been such as to initiate the student into the true value and force of the will in some of its higher aspects, his allegiance to and active work in the Order will surely demand this at no distant time. He will be thrown back upon his own inner strength in the very act of demanding that strength from the Master. I will give a concrete example: A member in this jurisdiction had reached a certain stage of the Temple lectures. He had received much encouragement from others in his studies, but ultimately resigned, alleging as his reason that the work lacked what he called the human element. This is the first instance I have known of a member giving this reason for his inability to progress. The facts of the case were these: The student was satisfied with what he termed "Rosicrucian principles," and admitted that he did not want any teaching beyond these—whatever the "principles" might be. He simply was not ready to accept the inner consequences of taking practical knowledge. His will was not equal to an advance; he was content to remain stationary, resting in a limited theoretical acceptance of certain fundamentals. This is not a case for criticism, but for clear understanding. It is an occasion for regret that a student who has expressed a strong wish for higher unfoldment should yet deliberately put aside the surest means for attainment. But just at the crucial point the law of elimination became operative and he was unable to proceed because of his unreadiness. If a student fears to take the consequence of enlightenment, prefers to remain upon the little platform of knowledge he has carefully measured and erected for himself, and stifles the voice of the soul which is actually urging him to larger issues, the door of opportunity is automatically closed and he must wait until a further cycle of experience has reinforced the mental faculties with greater strength and purpose. The law demands that a student must help himself.

Now the Brother Serapis, of the Egyptian Brotherhood, refers very specifically to this matter of energetic direction of the will: "For he who hopes to solve in time the great problems of the Macrocosmal World and conquer face to face the Dweller, taking thus by violence the threshold on which lie buried nature's most mysterious secrets, must Try, first, the energy of his Will Power, the indomitable resolution to succeed, and bringing out to light all the hidden mental faculties of his Atma and highest intelligence, get at the problem of Man's Nature and solve first the mysteries of the heart."

It is useless for us to attempt to shirk the issue by saying that the human element is lacking in phraseology of this kind. If we are still children and require our disciplinary instruction well sugared, nay, lived for us, the divine admonition of the Master will certainly prove too much for our human nature, and repel us. It is to be hoped that the majority of our members are beyond that stage; that the exigencies of life have compelled the assertion of their manhood; that they are aware of their deepest need and the need of their fellow men, and are not likely to turn back from the path they have studied and the truth they know because of what may appear to be a strain of severity in the word of the Master, which foreshadows a higher discipline and consequent renunciation perhaps of certain common interests

which have had their day and dissipate energy. There may be many a secret struggle between these interests and the graver aspect of truth which silently beckons us on. It cannot be otherwise in view of the strong momentum of un-spiritual mentation established during the long past in the subjective consciousness. Those of us who have persistently fought our way along certain hard phases of the path know well enough the painful misgivings, the harassing doubts, the solitary questionings of the heart, which have beset us; yet I believe there is not one of us but would testify, on emerging from the shadow, that it is well. What matters the difficulty if we have comprehended the way, the truth and the life that the Master offers us? Indeed, there is no other way by which the will can reach its strength, or the Master would certainly have told us. No matter to what Master we look for guidance, one admonition characterizes them all in regard to passing from our world into this: the necessity for the dominant force of the spiritual will is ever insisted upon.

The technique of the Master is pre-eminently active, not passive. Observe the leading thoughts of the above quotation: "Conquer: take by violence: try: indomitable resolution: bring out: get out." The whole process is one of intense inner action. I venture to affirm there is not a great character in universal history in which this supreme motive power is not seen to be a compelling factor. At first sight it may not always appear to be so; according to the manifold types and careers this central force of the awakened will may be strongly objective or more or less underlying, but it is there, organized, concentrated and potent. Only, on occult levels, a different order of experience ensues. The great character on the stage of world history does not necessarily enter consciously and with specific intent into the secret domain of the Spirit, his direction in life is technically unspiritual. Great as are his works in the manifold fields of human endeavor, strong as his ray of individual genius may be, he is not an occultist in the accepted sense of the term, nor

is he subject to the laws of the occult. The sovereign faculties of intuition and reason, developed to a rare degree, make him what he is. He is not engaged in a culture, the discipline of which would carry him beyond a certain exalted stage of human consciousness. The purely occult tests are withheld; from such he may as surely shrink as would the average human being.

Now, the Master exercises all the prerogative of genius, all the faculties of human consciousness in him are raised to their highest potency, and, in addition, the spiritual counterparts, so to speak, of these faculties, are operative and under perfect control, hence his vast authority, supreme value, and august ascendency over the higher manifestations of human genius. It is to the development of these deeper faculties, the spiritual counterparts of the finest faculties of human consciousness, that our attention as occult students is given, hence the note of severity which characterizes the discipline inculcated by the Master. And in attempting to pass beyond the frontiers of common worldly experience, no matter to what height of experience in any of its varied forms natural genius may have carried us within this experience, in the deliberate, conscious attempt to take the word of the Master and occultly speculate into the silent and mysterious domain of the Super Experience, the will is subjected to the finer and super-physical tests which are the unalterable laws of that domain. No man can offer himself sincerely as a candidate for his quest of the Spirit without setting up within certain powerful reactions of a peculiar and intimate character, which will surely try out what sort of man he is. It is the initial stage of a process of readjustment of all his values. There is nothing to be feared in the experience; it is a great privilege that he feels the call in his nature to meet it. Conscientious study and meditation should give him the necessary strength to meet it. It is not that he has to prepare to lose that which is dear and valuable to him, or renounce any talent or prestige he possesses in the world of men, or throw off any business or domestic obligations to which he is committed—not a word of this is written in the vocabulary of true occultism. He has simply to cultivate strength of will to realize himself as he is—which implies far more than we usually think, for when the force of concentrated will is focused steadily and over a long period upon the psychic and spiritual self, every motive and tendency buried in the heart of man is awakened to palpitating life and activity; all that Karma has written in his members arises and confronts him.

That is one phase of the great problem to which the admonition of the Master applies; and *there* it is, before that intimate personal disclosure of the man he is, that the student has to stand firm and undismayed in the face of much that he would hesitate to utter. Is there then any wisdom in averting the eyes from that which the Spirit demands that he should fearlessly confront and steadily overcome? We have called upon the name of the Master and the answer comes in the form of the vital refining fire that descends within to purge and purify every one of us who aspires after the hidden mysteries. Shall we weakly decline what we have deliberately invoked and postpone the blessed work of personal re-demption, because of the imminent possibility of the mortal self, which we love so well, being stretched sacrificially upon the cross which rises mystically on the path before us? Is there any tragedy in life like unto that in which a man, having taken knowledge of the way, retreats from the call of the Cosmic when the dark hour comes in which he must find his own light and press steadfastly on?

In my work in the Order it has been my privilege to have this problem again and again raised by students who have stood face to face with the shadow of the dark night of the soul, to which their strong and sincere effort on the path had brought them; and one of the greatest inspirations to me has been to note their firm grip on themselves, their philosophical stand in their trial, and the deep spiritual assurance they have had that all must be well and the goal would be reached. They are right. The Master's word has not gone forth for naught; and we can prove this by taking the austere ritual of the conquering will uttered by the Brother, and working it out in the silence, until all that is hidden in the inmost recesses of the heart is brought to light, and understood, and the baser metals transmitted into the pure gold of inner illumination.

▽ ▽ ▽ ▽ ▽

Notice to All Members

Within recent months, so many newspapers and magazines in North America have been publishing pictures, stories, and notations regarding Rosicrucian activities in America, and especially regarding the AMORC, that it has been almost impossible for our Editorial Department at Headquarters to keep up with the clipping and classification of these news items, because of our inability to discover quickly where and when such news items appear. We therefore ask our members to kindly send to us the clippings from any newspaper or magazine which they may read, which pertains to Rosicrucianism in general, or especially to the AMORC. When cutting such an item from a newspaper, please attach to it a little notation giving the name of the publication, and the date in which the article appeared. We will thank you for this splendid help in connection with our nationwide propaganda.

Waiting for The Master

By Raymund Andrea
Grand Master, AMORC, Great Britain

▽　▽　▽　▽　▽

IN the Ninth Grade we stand at the threshold of a greater life. We await the Master who is to initiate us into divine cognition and a knowledge of our true mission on the path. In this highly mystical grade there is significant pause and vast scope for contemplation. Looking back over the grades, it seems as if we had gradually ascended a great and narrowing stairway, step by step, and now stand on the last stair, far away from the voices of earth, before the portals of the unseen temple. Many have fallen away as the ascent grew steeper: the reward was too remote and the goal intangible. They fell away because they had not faith, and their portion will be a still continuing and unappeased hunger for that life which lies beyond the threshold which is approached in the Ninth Grade.

The pause and silence in the Ninth Grade constitute one of the greatest tests we have to meet on the path. We may have done all in our power, and the Master has not appeared. I know not why; I only know that in many lives the fact is so. Yet I feel convinced that there are certain conditions to be met, certain work to be accomplished, which we may dimly apprehend but which the Master knows, absolutely and in detail, are necessary for us to meet and to accomplish before we may share in his life. At this point we retain a firm footing through the exercise of an indomitable faith. I doubt whether one of us has come so far without realizing within, in one form or another, the strongest reason for this faith in those things which remain hidden to us just beyond the threshold. Those of us who have given the best part of our lives to the study and contemplation of higher things are seldom troubled with anxious questionings as to the path we have chosen, the reward of our effort, or the ultimate goal. We live onward from day to day in confidence that such aspects of truth and revelations of the divine as we are ready to accept and fitted to receive will be lawfully unfolded to an aspiring consciousness, and that veil after veil will pass away as we live and serve in the world of men. And it is inconceivable that those who entered upon the study of the path for the first time when they contacted the Order, passed through the grades understandingly, and now stand with us in the mystical pause of the Ninth Grade, have not the inner assurance of a reward for their labor and a realization of expanding consciousness. Their ability to demonstrate objectively may still be negligible; they may feel that they have little to show as a result of their study and meditation; yet experience warrants us in saying that such objective demonstration is by no means the only criterion of progress. It is just at this point in his studies that so much depends, in my opinion, on a student having a fairly clear idea of his inner status on the path. If he were studying in a certain course at the university with the hope of graduating for a specific profession, a time would ultimately arrive when he would need to take thorough stock of himself before presentation for examination to that end. He would need to gauge his weakness and his strength; he would submit to a careful self-examination and exercise himself in every way for qualification. Is not his position in the Ninth Grade somewhat analogous to this? But here he is largely his own instructor: he need entertain no fear of being "sent down" in the absence of certain qualifications. The period of waiting may be prolonged, but there is no failure.

This leads us to the important question of what is the outstanding qualification for passing beyond the threshold in the Ninth Grade. We are clearly confronted with no ordinary test. Upon entering each grade we have passed a threshold, at least symbolically. But at some stage of our progress through the Ninth Grade there is to be a definite translation of consciousness; during the interval of this grade we are engaged in a refining preparation which is to culminate in a complete change of polarity. Personally, I do not think this is to be achieved by any specific occult experiment, although some members in the Ninth Grade appear to hold this idea. I have often studied, with a good deal of interest, photographs depicting the remarkable throws of the proficient in ju jitsu; but woe to the man who attempts these if he has not a sufficiently athletic body and the requisite flexibility and strength of muscle and mental resources. There may not be the element of danger in the occult experiment that resides in the simple looking throw, but a vast amount of conscientious preparation is necessary in both cases.

There was a time when I could not altogether understand the urgent admonition of advanced occultists *to serve*. On more than one occasion when I had almost implored these greater souls of one school or another of occult teaching to give me some exceptional soul knowledge or instruction to satisfy the fierce hunger for advancement, I was uniformly pointed to the path of service. It was put to me most strongly that it was practically useless to engage in meditation and speculation about the soul unless the knowledge and force already possessed as the reward of past effort were communicated in some form for the assistance of others. Indeed, it was not until I contacted our Order that the significance of this admonition was fully realized and given effect.

It appears to be a condition of the threshold that the aspirant must retreat from the very point to which he has attained if he would go further. It seems that he is called upon to show in a very unique manner what sort of

man he is; and this is not, as we are apt to think, by some remarkable demonstration of divine or occult power, but rather in what measure he can work upon the souls of lesser aspirants and raise them, too, to this level of renunciation. And unless I am greatly mistaken, that is the keynote of the pause in the Ninth Grade. There must be some dominant characteristic in the nature of the aspirant which stamps him as a different man from his fellows—or surely the reality of his position in this grade is lost to him! That characteristic must be as the vital breath of the soul and radiate powerfully in the world of men. For, in a sense, no one has a right in the Ninth Grade unless he is willing to assume the responsibility of taking knowledge. That responsibility is, that he shall project the light he has into the darkness for the guidance of others. Failure lies in considering too critically and nicely the quality of the light possessed. Such as we have we must use—now, and be grateful that our earnest search for knowledge has kindled so much in the soul. The aspirant, in order to gain confidence in using the light he has need only reflect upon the multitudes around him, a good percentage of which would give nearly all they possess to have the knowledge and conviction about the deeper realities of life that he has. We are far too prone to think, because we have not some extraordinary insight into supersensible truth, or lack the facility of some admired exponent of it, or cannot immediately unravel every problem that confronts us and read the soul of man as an opened volume, that we must *wait* and do nothing. This will never satisfy the soul, nor prepare us for that which we must handle with strength and mastery when we pass beyond the threshold.

Here, then, we come face to face with the one qualification which overshadows all others and which must be brought out in the Ninth Grade. We have almost to forget the goal in inspiring others on the way to it. We have to cool ourselves of this fever for advancement which constantly tempts us to leap away on to the heights and stand there, conscious of our celestial radiance and elevation beyond the masses, only to *look down.* What use has a Master for a surveyor of human lives? This is one of the most prolific of the poisonous plants in the garden of modern occultism; it propagates serene and debonair souls, clothed in majestic repose and conscious meritoriousness, having a rosary of theories too sacred for utterance except among the elect, and far beyond the comprehension of this evil world, or any advanced soul in it who thinks not likewise. If that is *height,* they have the right to it since they sought and attained it; but if in some incarnation they happen to contact a Master I think the first admonition they will receive will be, to *come down.* And this is a hint for us if so be any of us have misinterpreted the way. We must do something with might and main for those who want what we have. We have to come down now to the problem of any soul that confronts us and wrestle with it, even though it be formidable and apparently far beyond us. We have no idea of the strength and range of our knowledge and power until we, with something akin to heroic passion, endeavor to use them. Surely, the past years of silent thought and meditation, and upward aspiring must be allowed to have fostered something in the soul worthy of use, or we have wasted precious time. We might have mastered a language or studied a literature as a desirable acquisition and a proof of culture, and taken infinite delight in a skillful expression of it in the associations of every day life. Yet this is insignificant in comparison with the secret forces of light and leading of which every true aspirant should be conscious and desire to manifest. If this seems a severe judgment, I can only say that I see no reason for speaking less unreservedly, since it touches the heart of our own particular problem of the threshold. Before we take serious knowledge of the way, our life may be as easy-going and indifferent as we choose to make it; others may have their problems and suffer under them, and there may be no inner compulsion on our part to

trouble much about them. It is the note of the world; and since we have to build for ourselves there appears nothing illogical in making our own path sure. *On the occult path this is a crime.* It will shut fast every avenue of approach to the life of the Masters. True, we must think for ourselves; a true knowledge of self and an endeavor to achieve a right adjustment to life must necessarily be a constant aim— but only that we might work the more skillfully and effectively upon the souls of our fellowmen for their advancement. A soul in pain — I use the words deliberately — will vibrate every living chord in the heart of a true Rosicrucian. He will forget conventions, rise beyond himself under the strong impulse of the will to enlighten and ameliorate, and pass into another soul without let or hindrance by the divine right of an understanding compassion, and that mystic and vital contact will have wrought in secret and never be forgotten.

This capital qualification, then, or self-exploitation for the assistance of others, has either to appear spontaneously in the soul of the aspirant before the threshold or must be cultured for with a no less conscientious laboriousness than that of an artist seeking to reflect the light and truth of ethereal nature across his canvas, or that of a writer laboring to embody immortal truth in language that wrings tears from human hearts. The personal self has to be laid upon the altar of service to living souls. Nothing less than this will suffice. Do we not plainly discern this stern, unrelenting, self-denying service in the Masters of men? That unearthly beauty and profound peace which they reflect are derived fundamentally from this one thing. If not, what else can give this majesty to mortal man? Nothing in the world, either in literature, art or science, or the path of life would be marshalled with angelic beings; whereas the flower of humanity is so rare that our life is one long yearning to encounter it. Some of us, at least, are only too well aware of this; we know what it is to greatly serve and we know that it calls for the right kind of soul. We

have seen many a path of lesser glory in the eyes of the Masters, but of great account in the eyes of the world, which we could have trodden and thereby seized just and coveted rewards, yet have renounced them until they now grow dim in the distance. It is well, and as it should be—for us. As surely as we await the Master, the Master waits for us, until the one decisive attitude is so firmly established as to preclude even the thought of sacrifice. Supreme dedication is the secret key in any great life. It is an extreme polarity which refuses to be biased by lesser things than the flaming ideal upon which the eyes are fixed. But on the occult path there is no violence, no forced development to this end. The service demanded by the Master is the full bloom of the soul, not the strained exertion of a disproportional development of any particular faculty. This is obvious; for when confronted with the problem of a soul we shall be little more than helpless before it if our life and knowledge have moved simply to one point and the problem be viewed merely from thence. The problem must become our problem and be viewed from the precise angle and altitude of the soul whose problem it is. We translate ourselves by inner and sympathetic contact.

I said, that the established attitude of service precludes even the thought of sacrifice. There may be something of the nature of a crucifixion of the personal self, but we cannot regard it as loss or deprivation. The increasing momentum of the outgoing force of the soul seems to overwhelm and obliterate, or shall we say, depolarize the personal factor. I should be more inclined to term it the way of loneliness than of crucifixion. One of the occult scriptures says: When the disciple has conquered the hunger of the heart, and refuses to live on the love of others, he finds himself more capable of in-

spiring love; when the heart no longer wishes to take, it is called upon to give abundantly. That is high doctrine, and perhaps we have not touched its level yet; but the approach thereto is not crucifixion—it is spiritual loneliness. And this particular stage of the path will be difficult to tread and its vibration hard to bear according to the native or acquired vigor of the soul for the quest. Certainly there is immense possibility in it, and here in the Ninth Grade I believe we are dealing with it. There are many references to this fact of loneliness in occult literature, yet, for all our theoretical knowledge of it, we are more or less disquieted in experiencing the solitudes of the path. What we have aspired to has in part been attained, and then we question the rightness of the attainment. But there is a never failing and tranquillizing thought upon which the aspirant can rest in such an exigency: whatever altered condition of mental aspect or conscious awareness of finding himself well out on a comparatively solitary path of investigation and remote from the common interests of men, whatever inner questionings may arise as to further pursuit of an uncommon enterprise which lesser souls are only too ready to pronounce unprofitable and discourage him from, he will know that a higher and subtler strength is of greater value in evolution than a lower one, and when he becomes fully adjusted to it he will be capable of the greater works of that higher strength. Remember, it will be impossible to contact and hold the intense vibration of life beyond the threshold without this specific culture of the vibration within ourselves. To this end we labor. We seek to touch the super-levels of consciousness, and as the growing pains we have to experience and the intervals of loneliness that test us in the ascent are necessary and unavoidable, let us hold steadfastly on until the Master appears.

▽ ▽ ▽ ▽ ▽

Lightning Source UK Ltd.
Milton Keynes UK
UKOW05f1946250717

306043UK00005B/251/P

9 781163 073599